A PARRAGON BOOK
Published by Parragon Books, Unit 13-17 Avonbridge Trading Estate,
Atlantic Road, Avonmouth, Bristol BS11 9QD
Produced by The Templar Company plc, Pippbrook Mill,
London Road, Dorking, Surrey RH4 1JE

Designed by Janie Louise Hunt
Edited by Caroline Steeden
Printed and bound in Italy
ISBN 1-85813-673-3

THE FIRST BOOK OF

Kings and Queens

WRITTEN BY CAROLINE STEEDEN
ILLUSTRATED BY HEMESH ALLES

‖ •PARRAGON• ‖

DATES OF ACCESSION

1066	**William** (the Conqueror)	1327	**Edward III**
1087	**William II**	1377	**Richard II**
1100	**Henry I**	1399	**Henry IV**
1135	**Stephen**	1413	**Henry V**
1154	**Henry II**	1422	**Henry VI**
1189	**Richard I**	1461	**Edward IV**
1199	**John**	1483	**Edward V**
1216	**Henry II**	1483	**Richard III**
1272	**Edward I**	1485	**Henry VII**
1307	**Edward II**	1509	**Henry VIII**

1547	Edward VI	1714	George I
1553	Jane	1727	George II
1553	Mary	1760	George III
1558	Elizabeth I	1820	George IV
1603	James I	1830	William IV
1625	Charles I	1837	Victoria
1649	Commonwealth	1901	Edward VII
1660	Charles II	1910	George V
1685	James II	1936	Edward VIII
1689	William and Mary	1936	George VI
1702	Anne	1952	Elizabeth II

WILLIAM the CONQUEROR
1066–1087

William the Conqueror was crowned king on Christmas Day 1066, at Westminster Abbey. He had claimed the throne after defeating King Harold II's Saxon army at the Battle of Hastings.

William had come to England from France, with his Norman supporters. Although some parts of the country readily accepted William as king, in other parts there was fierce opposition, and the Norman army had to build

castles from which to rule. Land was taken from the Saxon lords and given to Norman noblemen. In return the noblemen promised to support the king and provide him with an army. This system was called feudalism.

In 1067 work began on the Bayeaux Tapestry, a famous tapestry telling the story of the Norman conquest of England.

In 1086, William ordered a survey to be drawn up of every city, town and village in his kingdom, as well as a list of the people who lived there and the livestock they owned. This became known as the Domesday Book.

William died aged about 60, after an accident riding in battle left him seriously ill. He was very fond of hunting and created a large forest in Hampshire which he stocked with deer. He called it the New Forest.

WILLIAM II 1087–1100

On his death bed, William the Conqueror appointed his second son, William, as king. He was a good leader and an excellent soldier, but he was unpopular because of his extravagant lifestyle, and for cheating the Church of money. He built castles along the frontiers of Wales and Scotland, to guard against invasion.

He was killed by an arrow whilst hunting in the New Forest, and there was some doubt over whether this was 'accidental'.

He was buried in Winchester Cathedral, directly below the main tower. He never married and had no children.

HENRY I 1100–1135

Following his brother William's death, Henry was elected king. His elder brother Robert was away on a Crusade when William was killed. On returning, Robert claimed the crown, but his army was defeated by Henry, and he spent the rest of his life in prison.

Henry was a man of peace, and ruled wisely. He was well-educated and respected by his subjects.

His only legitimate son drowned in a shipwreck, which led to chaos and civil war upon Henry's death, as there were two contenders for the throne. He had chosen his daughter, Empress Matilda. But his nephew Stephen also had a claim to the throne…

STEPHEN 1135–1154

Stephen was a weak and ineffectual man, but when Henry died he claimed the throne, and with the support of his brother the Bishop of Winchester, the Church and the people, he was crowned king before Matilda could return to England. However, Matilda gathered enough support to challenge Stephen, and a civil war began, which lasted for many years and caused widespread death and destruction.

In 1144 Stephen lost Normandy to Matilda's husband, Geoffrey of Anjou, who was proclaimed duke. The powerful English barons persuaded Stephen to decide on his successor. The barons owned land in Normandy as well as England, and did not want to offend the new duke and his wife, so they persuaded the king to declare Matilda's son Henry as heir to the throne.

Stephen died the following year.

HENRY II
1154–1189

Henry II was a well-educated and powerful king. He was physically strong with a passionate, and sometimes bad-tempered nature. He was a determined leader, restoring law and order, driving the Scots out of England and invading North Wales.

He appointed his friend Thomas Becket as Archbishop of Canterbury, hoping he would help resolve an argument between Henry and the Church. But pleasure-seeking Thomas became a solemn, religious man. He sided with the Church against Henry, and had to flee the country. He returned in 1170 and Henry's exasperation led him to say to some of his knights, "Will no one rid me of this turbulent priest." Unbeknown to him, some of the knights did just that, riding to Canterbury and murdering Thomas in his own cathedral. Henry was struck with sorrow and remorse at the loss of his friend, and publicly did penance at his tomb.

The end of Henry's reign was taken up by quarrels with his sons, who joined rebellions against him, wishing to gain power for themselves. In 1189 Henry II discovered his sons had joined forces with King Phillip of France against him, and shortly afterwards he died of a broken heart.

RICHARD THE LIONHEART

1189–1199

Richard I was the eldest surviving son and undisputed heir of Henry II. He was known as 'the Lionheart' because of his bravery on the battlefield.

He spent little time in England during his reign, as he was away in the Holy Land fighting against the Moslems, leaving William Longchamp, Bishop of Ely, to rule the country in his absence. Richard and other European rulers made it their Crusade to return Jerusalem to Christian rule.

Returning from the Crusade, Richard was shipwrecked in the Adriatic Sea. He attempted to cross Europe by land, but was captured by the Duke of Austria, whom he had unwisely insulted in the Holy Land, and was kept prisoner for fifteen months.

In his absence his brother John declared him dead and tried to claim the throne, but finally the ransom money was raised, and Richard returned to England in 1194. A few months later he left for France, to defend his territories there which were under attack. He never returned to England, but died in France in 1199, after being injured by an enemy crossbow, and was buried at Fontevraud.

JOHN
1199–1216

Richard I named John as successor on his deathbed. But another contender for the throne was his nephew Arthur, who was only 11. John was supported by the noblemen, who didn't want a boy ruler, and a few years later, Arthur was mysteriously murdered, it was assumed on John's orders.

John had his first marriage annulled, and married twelve-year-old Isabella of Angoulême, with whom he had many children.

John was widely thought of as a cruel, greedy and violent king, though he could be merciful and generous. He was hated by his barons, as he ruled like a tyrant, and took money from the people to defend his French territories. However, he lost almost all of his father's huge empire in France.

In 1215, the barons rose up against him, aided by the Archbishop of Canterbury. They drew up a charter, which was a list of rules on how to govern the country, and King John sealed it at Runnymede. It was called the Magna Carta and is now kept at the British Museum.

The barons still did not trust him, and called in Louis of France, inviting him to take the throne. A civil war followed, which continued until John became ill and died in 1216. He was buried in Worcester Cathedral, where his tomb can still be seen today.

HENRY III
1216–1272

Henry was only nine years old when his father died and the throne passed to him. Hubert de Burgh was appointed as Regent, and ruled on his behalf until 1227 when Henry came of age.

Henry was a weak ruler, and infuriated the people by appointing friends and family to important positions. He spent large amounts of money unsuccessfully trying to regain lost lands in France, and he paid for this by raising taxes. The lay barons of the kingdom rose against him, and found a leader in Simon de Montfort, Earl of Leicester. They defeated Henry at the battle of Lewes in 1264. Simon became very powerful and virtually ruled the land, but the king's son, Edward, continued to lead the opposition. Simon de Montfort was killed at the battle of Evesham in 1265, and the king was returned to power, although it was Edward who took over governing the country. The last few years of Henry's reign were very peaceful.

Henry was a bad king, but he was not a bad man. He was well educated and was a great patron of the arts. Salisbury Cathedral was built during his reign, and Westminster Abbey was rebuilt, and it was there he was buried in 1272.

EDWARD I 1272–1307

Edward I was an outstanding king. Tall, strong and good-looking, he was a great soldier and a wise king. He had a high regard for justice and law, and his reforms laid the foundations of parliamentary government. He was a loving and faithful husband to Eleanor of Castile who accompanied him on crusades, once he had restored peace to England. He conquered Wales in 1283, and attempted several times to conquer Scotland. He died of dysentery at Carlisle whilst preparing to invade for the fourth time.

EDWARD II 1307–1327

Edward II was his parents' thirteenth child, and the only son to survive infancy. He was a weak-willed and rather pathetic man, greatly influenced by his friends, especially his favourite, Piers Gaveston. In 1314 Edward attempted to conquer the Scots, leading to a battle at Bannockburn against an army led by King Robert the Bruce. The English were defeated, with the loss of three thousand men. Edward was married to Isabella of France. In 1325 she went to France and joined the king's enemies.

They attacked England, and overthrew the king, who was taken to Berkley Castle, and murdered.

EDWARD III 1327–1377

Edward III was only fourteen when his father was murdered, and so the country was ruled by his mother and her lover, Roger Mortimer, until he came of age. He married and had a son, known as the Black Prince.

Through his mother, Edward had a strong claim to the French throne, and he began an attack on France, which became known as the Hundred Years War. At first he enjoyed great success, capturing the Channel, Calais, and the south-west of France, but later lost all the land he had conquered.

He was a strong and popular leader. He ordered the execution of Mortimer for the murder of his father, and had his mother held captive for the rest of her life.

During his reign the Black Death swept through England, killing almost half of the population. The Black Prince died of dysentery in 1376, and the king died a year later, by then a shambling and senile old man.

RICHARD II
1377–1399

Richard was the son of the Black Prince, and was ten when he became king. The country was governed by a group of twelve men, led by his uncle, John of Gaunt, Duke of Lancaster.

In 1381 the Peasants' Revolt, led by Wat Tyler, descended on London. Fired by the labour shortage following the Black Death, and the atmosphere of deep social unrest, the people rose up against the introduction of a poll tax. The king managed to pacify them, and restore law and order, bringing peace and better conditions to the country, and he enjoyed a period of popularity.

He married Anne of Bohemia, was deeply in love with her and was beside himself with grief when she died.

In 1396 Richard established peace with France, cementing it by marrying seven-year-old Isabella of France. However, more trouble was close at hand. His cousin, Henry Bolingbroke, Duke of Lancaster, whom he had sent into exile ten years previously, raised an army and recaptured the land Richard had taken from him. They dethroned the king, imprisoning him in Pontefract Castle, where he starved to death in 1400.

HENRY IV 1399–1413

Henry was the first Lancastrian King. He was the son of John of Gaunt and the nephew of Richard II, but was not the rightful heir. His reign was an uneasy one, with battles against the Welsh, Scots and French. Until 1405 there were constant rebellions and civil wars. Henry dealt with the rebels ruthlessly, executing them and displaying their bodies as a warning to others.

Plagued by guilt over his treatment of Richard II, he died in 1413 a bitter, troubled and sick man. He was buried in Canterbury Cathedral.

HENRY V 1413–1422

The eldest son of Henry IV was a clever, gifted man. He restored peace to the country, securing his subjects' loyalty and the support of the nobles by uniting them in a renewal of the war against France, begun by Edward III. He was successful on the battlefield and in 1415 won a great victory at the Battle of Agincourt, where his men rained arrows on the French soldiers, who were bogged down in the mud by their heavy armour.

He captured Normandy and by 1419 English forces had reached Paris. Peace talks led to the Treaty of Troyes, recognizing Henry as heir to the French throne, and he married the French king's daughter. Two years later Henry and the French king died, leaving Henry's baby son to rule both countries.

HENRY VI
1422–1461 and 1470–1471

Henry VI came to the throne aged eight months, younger than any other English sovereign. He was crowned King of England on his eighth birthday, and King of France two years later. His uncles ruled until he was old enough take over. He was a rather weak character and suffered from bouts of insanity throughout his life.

In 1445 he married Margaret of Anjou, who was as strong as he was weak. Whilst he was ill, Richard, Duke of York, reigned as protector, but on Henry's recovery, the queen and the Duke of Somerset took control. Richard had a stronger claim to the throne than Henry, and soon open warfare broke out between the rival Lancastrians and Yorkists, with each side claiming the throne. The battles were known as the Wars of the Roses, as the Lancastrians had the red rose as their symbol and the Yorkists the white. Many lives were lost, including Richard's, whose son Edward became the new Duke of York. After defeating the Lancastrians at the Battle of Towton, Edward was crowned king. Henry was captured in 1465, and spent the remainder of his life in the Tower of London, apart from a brief spell following further battles, when he was reinstated as king. He was murdered at the Tower in 1471.

EDWARD IV 1461–1470 and 1471–1483

Following the Battle of Towton Edward was crowned king. Tall, handsome and charming, he enjoyed London society, and was a popular king. He lived in luxury, having acquired the wealth of the noblemen killed in battle.

Battles continued against the Lancastrians throughout his reign. At one point he was beaten by the Duke of Warwick, and fled to France. Henry VI briefly regained the throne, but before long Edward returned, and following the deaths of both Henry and his son, the threat of a Lancastrian claim to the throne was removed.

He married Elizabeth Woodville, and had ten children. On his death he willed that his eldest son succeed him, and that until he came of age, his brother Richard, Duke of Gloucester, should be Protector.

EDWARD V 1483

Edward V was twelve years old when his father died and he became king. But before he could be crowned his parents' marriage was declared invalid by the Bishop of Bath and Wells, making him illegitimate and therefore unable to inherit the crown. The throne was offered to his uncle, who was crowned Richard III. A great mystery surrounds Edward and his younger brother, who were kept in the Tower. After the coronation neither of them were ever seen again, nor their bodies found. The most popular theory is that they were smothered to death in their sleep on the orders of Richard III, but we shall probably never discover the truth.

RICHARD III 1483–1485

After his coronation, Richard met with hostility from all sides. Despite attempts to win support, feelings ran high against him. Owing largely to the efforts of the Tudor propagandists, Richard's reputation as an evil, murderous hunchback has persisted until recently. A fairer picture of him has emerged, as an honest king, brave soldier and a loving husband. His only son died aged ten, and his wife, Anne, followed a year later.

The Lancastrians rallied against him under Henry Tudor. In 1485 Henry met Richard in battle at Bosworth, and a fierce fight led to Richard's death, still wearing his crown. It was taken from him and placed on Henry's head, bringing the Wars of the Roses to an end, and the Tudor period into being.

HENRY VII
1485–1509

Henry was born three months after the death of his father, Edmund Tudor. He grew up to lead the Lancastrians against Richard III at the Battle of Bosworth in 1485. Following Richard's defeat, Henry was crowned king, and went on to marry Elizabeth of York, thus uniting the rival houses of Lancaster and York.

Henry was determined to restore peace and order to the nation. He was an orderly man and ruled wisely and firmly. With heavy taxes and fines, he reduced the wealth of the nobles, and brought the struggles between the Crown and the barons to an end. He made trading treaties with Europe, and by encouraging industry brought prosperity both for himself and his people.

During his reign Henry had to deal with two pretenders to the throne, Lambert Simnel, and Perkin Warbeck, who claimed to be one of the princes in the tower. Henry tried to unite England and Scotland, by marrying his daughter to King James IV of Scotland, bringing peace during his reign.

Henry was probably the most able businessman to sit on the throne, and when he died at his new palace in Richmond in 1509, he left the country in peace and prosperity.

HENRY VIII
1509–1547

Following his brother Arthur's death, Henry became heir to the throne, and when he became king, he married Arthur's widow, Catherine of Aragon. Henry was well educated and a gifted poet, musician, athlete and artist. He recommended war with France, and saw off a Scots invasion at Flodden Field. He relied heavily on his close friend Thomas Wolsey, who effectively ruled the realm.

Catherine bore Henry six children, but only one girl survived. Desperate for a male heir Henry decided to divorce her. However, they were Catholics, and despite Wolsey's efforts, the Pope would not annul the marriage. This lead to Henry's break with the Catholic Church, the Reformation in England with the king declared head of the Church, and the dismissal of Wolsey as Chancellor. Archbishop Cranmer declared Henry's marriage invalid, and he married Anne Boleyn. She bore him a daughter and a stillborn son. Convicted of adultery, she was beheaded, leaving Henry free to marry Jane Seymour. In the same year, the monasteries' wealth was seized, Church property was sold, and the money went to the Treasury.

Jane died giving birth to the long-awaited male heir, Edward, and soon afterwards Henry made a political marriage to Anne of Cleves. He soon regretted this marriage, however, and had it annulled.

His fifth wife, Catherine Howard, was nearly thirty years younger than the by now ailing king. Henry had grown very fat, was prematurely senile, had gout and an ulcerated leg. Catherine was unfaithful and, convicted of adultery, was beheaded. Henry's sixth, and final wife, Catherine Parr, nursed him until he died in 1547, leaving behind him a united and secure nation.

Catherine of Aragon

Anne Boleyn

Jane Seymour

Anne of Cleves

Catherine Howard

Catherine Parr

EDWARD VI 1547–1553

Edward, Henry's only son, inherited the throne aged ten, at a time when the country was very unsettled. Religious fanaticism was at a peak, and there were great power struggles between the Protestant and Catholic Church.

Edward was brought up by nurses and tutors and became very scholarly. His protector, the Duke of Somerset, mismanaged the economy, which resulted in his execution in an uprising led by Thomas Ket. The Duke of Northumberland took his place as Protector, but his over-ambition soon led to his downfall.

Edward was a sickly child. By the age of fifteen it became clear he would not survive much longer. Northumberland married his son to Lady Jane Grey, and persuaded Edward to name her as his heir. Soon after Edward died, and the throne passed to Jane.

JANE   JULY 1553

Lady Jane Grey had little interest in being queen, and only held the title for nine days. A staunch Protestant, she was overthrown by Mary Tudor, a fierce Catholic who had the support of the people. Lady Jane was executed along with her husband and father-in-law for treason.

MARY 1553–1558

Mary Tudor was the only child of Henry VIII and Catherine of Aragon to survive infancy. She had a difficult childhood, suffering with ill health as a result of a disease inherited from her father. She was persecuted for being a devout Catholic like her mother, and suffered the shame of being declared illegitimate, although she was later reinstated to the line of succession.

On succeeding the throne she embarked on a fanatical mission to restore Catholicism, earning herself the nickname of 'Bloody Mary', as she had about three hundred Protestants burnt at the stake for refusing to convert. She abolished Edward VI's religious laws, but could not restore land to the Catholic Church which had previously been taken from it.

She married the Catholic Prince Philip of Spain, and joined him in a war against France, which resulted in the loss of Calais. However the marriage only lasted fourteen months, and Mary was devastated when Philip left her and returned to Spain. She died in 1558, a sad, pathetic, unloved woman, leaving behind her a country with deep religious divisions.

ELIZABETH I
1558–1603

Elizabeth came to the throne following the death of Mary. The Catholics refused to accept her as queen at first, as her mother, Anne Boleyn, had been divorced. Elizabeth was a Protestant, however, and set about re-establishing the Protestant faith with great determination.

Her cousin Mary, Queen of Scots, had fled to England and Elizabeth kept her hidden away for twenty years, until Catholic plots to depose Elizabeth and put Mary on the throne in her place forced her to charge Mary with treason and sentence her to death. Europe's Catholic monarchs were furious, and the Spanish Armada, a huge fleet of ships, attacked England. But Spain's ships were no match for the brilliant tactics and experience of the English fleet, led by Francis Drake, who was later knighted as the first Englishman to sail around the world. The Elizabethan Age was one of adventure. Sir Walter Raleigh sailed to America, bringing back tobacco and potatoes.

Elizabeth loved elaborate dress and jewels and refused to admit to ageing. In later life she wore a huge red wig and a lot of make-up. She was courted by foreign princes and English noblemen, but never married and produced no heir. She ruled wisely, with the help of many well chosen advisers, and before she died named James VI of Scotland, son of Mary, Queen of Scots, as her heir.

She died at Richmond Palace, in 1603, and a messenger set out at once for Scotland to give the new King James the news.

JAMES I
1603–1625

James Stuart was only a year old when his mother Mary, Queen of Scots, abdicated and fled Scotland, leaving him behind as King James VI. Alongside his wife, Anne of Denmark, he was crowned King of England in 1603, and was the first king to rule both countries.

Freed from the restrictive power of the Scottish nobles and clergy, James set out to assert his authority, promoting his theory of the 'divine right of kings', that the king was above the law and answerable only to God. He fought constantly with Parliament, and ruled without one for many years.

In 1605 there was a Catholic plot to blow up the Protestant king at the opening of Parliament on November 5th. Guy Fawkes was caught about to set fire to a trail of gunpowder, and was later beheaded. During his reign, Sir Walter Raleigh was also beheaded, at the insistence of Spain.

James was not a popular king, infuriating the people by promoting his favourites, such as the Duke of Buckingham, to powerful posts. He was

given the nickname 'the wisest fool in Christendom', as despite being
well-educated and intelligent, he was also ill-mannered, coarse and cowardly.

CHARLES I
1625–1649

Charles was James's second son, but inherited the throne as his elder brother had died of typhoid some years earlier. He was a great patron of the Arts, and was handsome, charming and popular. He married Henrietta Maria of France, and the first years of his reign were happy ones. However, he, like his father, believed in his divine right to rule, and he dismissed Parliament following their refusal to grant him money for foreign wars. He ruled without them for eleven years until, in 1640, he was forced to summon them again. Once more the king clashed with Parliament, and matters came to a head when Charles entered the House of Commons with an armed guard to arrest the members he saw as the chief troublemakers. Civil war broke out, and the country divided in support of the two sides. Charles' supporters were the Royalists, and were known as the Cavaliers. Parliament's supporters were the Parliamentarians, led by Oliver Cromwell, and were known as the Roundheads, because of their short haircuts. In 1645 the Cavaliers were finally defeated by the Roundheads at the battle of Naseby. After an imprisonment in Carisbrook Castle, Charles was tried and sentenced to death, which was duly carried out in 1649 when he was beheaded.

41

COMMONWEALTH 1649–1660

The period known as the Commonwealth was an interregnum, which means the period between two reigns, and during that time England was a republic. Oliver Cromwell was leader of the Parliamentarians, but frequently disagreed with his followers. Eventually he dissolved Parliament and declared himself as Lord Protector. His puritanical laws led to virtual civil war, and after his death in 1558, his son was unable to keep control. Charles I's eldest son took the throne as Charles II.

CHARLES II 1660–1685

Charles was handsome, good-humoured and charming. Following his coronation in 1661, he re-opened the theatres, which had been closed under puritanical rule, and singing and dancing were once again allowed. He restored Parliament, the House of Lords, the Catholic Church and the Cavalier gentry. His broad education was both practical and sensible. He married Catherine of Braganza from Portugal, who brought a dowry of £300,000 and the naval bases of Tangier and Bombay. Charles also had mistresses, the most famous being Nell Gwynne, and had many illegitimate children, although his marriage remained childless.

The Great Plague of London took place in 1665, followed by the Great Fire the next year. There was still a lot of religious tension. Protestants tried to ban Charles from naming his brother as heir. But they failed, and when Charles died, the throne passed to James.

JAMES II 1685–1689
When James II succeeded his brother, he infuriated Parliament by appointing Catholics to senior posts. His religious fervour was tolerated, because his heir was his Protestant daughter Mary, who was married to William of Orange. Charles II's eldest illegitimate son, James, Duke of Monmouth, led a Protestant rebellion, but was defeated at Sedgemoor, and executed along with hundreds of other rebels in the 'Bloody Assizes'.

James's first wife died, leaving him with two daughters, Mary and Anne. His second wife had no surviving children, until in 1688, she had a son, who became heir to the throne. Protestant conspirators asked William of Orange to invade England, which he did, and King James II was forced to flee to France. He returned to face William once more at the Battle of the Boyne, in Ireland, but was again defeated and returned to France, never to set foot in England again.

WILLIAM and MARY 1689–1702

Although Mary was the true successor to the throne, she had promised her husband, William of Orange, that he could rule jointly with her when the time came. Following the Battle of the Boyne, when William's troops beat King James II's, that time arrived as James was forced to flee to France. Mary died of smallpox in 1694, and William continued to rule alone.

The couple did not have any children, and there was some concern over who would succeed them, but before William's death he arranged for Mary's sister, Anne, to inherit the throne. He also signed the Act of Settlement which barred Catholics from succeeding to the throne after Anne's death.

William died in 1702, following a bad fall from his horse when it stumbled on a mole hill.

ANNE 1702–1714

Queen Anne was the last of the Stuart monarchs. She was married to the Prince of Denmark, who was considered rather boring. Anne was kind, gentle, and warm-hearted, but had little interest in State affairs. One of the most important events during her reign was the signing of the Act of Union, uniting the Scottish and English parliaments, and bringing Great Britain officially into being. Anne suffered from poor health throughout her life, and had an appalling maternity record, with eighteen pregnancies in sixteen years producing only five living children, none of whom survived childhood. She died in 1714, after a series of strokes, and was so stout that her massive coffin was almost square.

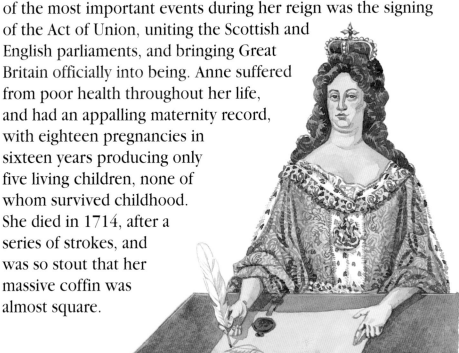

GEORGE I 1714–1727

As Queen Anne had no heir, she decided that the Electress Sophia of Hanover, granddaughter of James I and VI, should inherit the throne on her death. But she died two months before Anne, and so it was her son George who was crowned king in 1714. He spoke virtually no English and did not like England, spending most of his time in Germany, which is why Robert Walpole was appointed to take his place in Parliament. He is often referred to as the first Prime Minister. George's reign was quiet, apart from some trouble with the Jacobites who were trying to reinstate a Catholic king, but were defeated.

George had divorced his wife twenty years before he became king, and kept her imprisoned until her death. There was great hostility between George and his son. He died in 1727 whilst travelling to Hanover.

Robert Walpole

GEORGE II 1727–1760

George II came to the throne following the death of his father, and was a more easy-going and popular king, speaking English with a heavy German accent. He led Britain in European wars against the French and Spanish. His reign was a time of prosperity for Britain, during which India and Canada were added to the British Empire. He was devoted to his wife, Caroline of Ansbach, and was buried in a grave adjoining hers at Westminster Abbey when he died in 1760.

GEORGE III
1760–1820

George III was the grandson of George II, his father having died before the king. He came to the throne during a highly prosperous period, and enjoyed a long and happy reign. He married a German princess, Charlotte, who bore him fifteen children, and they lived a simple life, residing for the main part at Buckingham House (now Palace), which George bought for £21,000 in 1762.

George III ruled firmly, removing the Cabinet and choosing his own ministers. In America the colonists were furious over the huge taxes put on American imports, and so disguised as Indians, they boarded some British ships which had arrived with a cargo of tea, and poured the tea into Boston Harbour. This became known as the Boston Tea Party, and was eventually to lead to the American War of Independence, as a result of which George's government collapsed and the Cabinet was reinstated, with William Pitt as Prime Minister. The French Revolution also took place during his reign, and the Napoleonic wars were fought in Europe.

George III took great interest in the changes in agriculture which were occurring, known as the Agricultural Revolution, and had the nickname of 'Farmer George'.

He suffered from bouts of madness throughout his life, brought about by an illness called porphyria, and spent his last years at Windsor, blind, deaf and mad. He died in 1820, having reigned for sixty years.

GEORGE IV
1820–1830

George IV was proclaimed Prince Regent in 1811, ruling the country throughout the last years of the incapacitated king's life. Following his father's death he was crowned king, and in keeping with his character his coronation was a lavish affair. George IV was a very flamboyant character, quite the opposite of his quiet, steady father. From an early age he developed a love of riotous living, gambling, drinking, and horse-racing and had affairs with a string of older women, the most famous of whom was Mrs Fitzherbert, whom he married in 1785. The marriage was annulled however, as she was Catholic and had been married twice before. George had very expensive tastes, and had repeatedly fallen badly into debt. He spent vast amounts on his first residence, Carlton House, and later built the Brighton Pavilion. There was a great deal of poverty at this time, as the war with France was funded by high taxes, and George's extravagance infuriated the population.

He was forced to marry his cousin, Caroline of Brunswick, in order to produce an heir, but they took an instant dislike to each other and the marriage was a disaster. They separated shortly after the birth of their only daughter, who died eighteen years later in childbirth, and George's attempts to divorce his wife added to his unpopularity with the people. He died in 1830, following a period of illness, and the throne passed to his brother.

WILLIAM IV
1830–1837

William came to the throne at the age of sixty-five, and his was to be a short-lived, but successful reign. He had spent most of his life at sea, working his way up through the ranks to become Admiral of the Fleet in 1811. During his naval career he had travelled extensively throughout the world, had seen active service, serving under Nelson's command. He was known fondly as 'the Sailor King'. Throughout his many years spent at sea he had developed a gruff and rather blunt manner, speaking his mind regardless of consequences. The people liked this down-to-earth approach, and he enjoyed great popularity.

During William's reign the Great Reform Act was passed by Parliament, giving many more middle-class men the vote.

Before he became heir to the throne William lived with his mistress, an actress called Mrs Jordan, and over a period of twenty years together they had ten children. However, in 1818, he married Adelaide of Saxe-Meiningen, who was later to be crowned Queen Adelaide, alongside her husband. She too enjoyed great popularity, having a gentle, sweet nature. Sadly, their only child to survive birth lived for just three months, the queen devoting her time instead to her illegitimate step-children, and when William died in 1837, the throne passed to his young niece, Victoria.

VICTORIA
1837–1901

Victoria was the granddaughter of George III, and came to the throne at the age of eighteen. She was the longest reigning British monarch, and saw great changes to the country in her sixty-four years on the throne, during which time Britain changed from a simple, rural society to a modern, industrial one.

In 1840 she married Prince Albert of Saxe-Coburg, with whom she was deeply in love. They had nine children, and the family enjoyed many happy times together at the homes Albert bought — Osborne House and Balmoral Castle.

Victoria and Albert worked hard for the country, and Britain became a powerful force throughout the world, expanding her Empire to include New Zealand, South Africa and India. There were ten prime ministers during her reign, including Palmerston, Gladstone and Disraeli. Many Acts were passed, education was made free and compulsory, income tax was introduced, trade unions were formed and the Labour Party was founded.

In 1851, Albert organised the Great Exhibition in Hyde Park, building the Crystal Palace to house the displays of machinery, manufactured goods, and technology. Profits from the exhibition were spent acquiring land in Kensington to build permanent museums of science and art, all of which remain, most notably the Victoria and Albert museum.

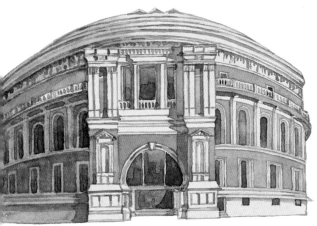

The Royal Albert Hall was built after Albert died of typhoid at the age of forty-two in 1861. Queen Victoria mourned him so deeply that she retreated from public life for almost all of the remaining forty years of her reign, refusing to attend even State occasions. She died in 1901, aged eighty-two.

EDWARD VII
1901–1910

Edward VII was nearly sixty by the time he came to the throne. During his mother's reign he had been completely excluded from any political involvement and had no experience of government, however he was to enjoy a successful reign as a very popular king. He was a charming man, who liked to indulge in good food, wine, cigars and company, especially the company of ladies. In his youth this pleasure-seeking attitude led him into some measure of scandal, and caused his parents great concern. Upon his succession however, it was his charm and diplomacy which earned him the nickname of 'Edward the Peacemaker', following his conclusion of the 'Entente Cordiale' with France, when he persuaded the French to agree to an alliance.

A couple of days before his coronation he was struck down with acute appendicitis, and had to have an operation, which delayed the ceremony by about six weeks. He was married to Alexandra of Denmark, and they had six children, enjoying many happy times at the house he bought at

Sandringham in Norfolk. He died in 1910, following a short illness, and was buried at St George's Chapel, Windsor. The nation was aware that the king's influence had maintained peace in Europe, and that that peace could soon be under threat.

GEORGE V 1910–1936

George's elder brother Albert had died in 1892, and so when King Edward died, George succeeded his father. George married Mary of Tech, who had been Albert's fiancé. She was well suited to George, and he was devoted to her.

He spent fifteen years in the navy before coming to the throne, and had a down-to-earth manner which endeared him to the people. He was well respected and became one of our best loved kings.

During his reign he witnessed many dramatic events, including the First World War. The British Empire survived, but by 1931 so many of the countries had become independent that it was renamed the British Commonwealth.

In 1935 King George V celebrated his Silver Jubilee, only to die the following year, and be succeeded by his son Edward.

EDWARD VIII 1936

Edward had been tremendously popular as the Prince of Wales. However, he had fallen in love with a twice-divorced woman, and it was clear upon his succession that she could never be accepted as queen. Forced to choose, he abdicated in favour of his brother and married her. They lived in France for the rest of their lives, as the Duke and Duchess of Windsor.

GEORGE VI 1936–1952

As the second son, Albert, Duke of York had never expected to become king. Like his father he had enjoyed a long naval career, and had seen active service in the First World War. He was a shy, nervous man, with delicate health and a speech impediment which made him stutter.

In 1923 he married Lady Elizabeth Bowes-Lyon, better known today as the Queen Mother. They had two daughters, Elizabeth and Margaret-Rose, and had a happy family life. Edward's abdication came as a terrible blow, but the family adjusted to their new position, and enjoyed immense popularity with the people. They greatly boosted public morale during the Second World War, refusing to leave London throughout the bombing, or to send their children away.

Sadly, shortly after the war was over the king's health began to deteriorate, and he was diagnosed as having lung cancer. In 1952 he died peacefully in his sleep, and his daughter Elizabeth came to the throne.

ELIZABETH II

1952–

Our present Queen was born on April 21st 1926. When she was born no one expected her to one day become Queen, but following her uncle Edward VIII's abdication, her father became king and she became heir to the throne. She spent most of the war years living at Windsor Castle, and was educated privately. In 1945, anxious to make a practical contribution to the war effort, she joined the Auxiliary Transport Service, studying car mechanics.

After the war she went on a tour of South Africa with her parents, and it was there that she celebrated her twenty-first birthday, marked by a speech broadcast to the Commonwealth pledging her life to its service. She fell in love with Prince Philip Mountbatten of Greece and Denmark and they were married in 1947. It was while on a tour of Kenya in 1952 that Elizabeth received the news of her father's death, and her succession. Winston Churchill was then Prime Minister, and the forty-two years of her reign have seen plenty of political upheaval since then. At that time most Commonwealth countries were ruled by Britain, although most have now won their independence. As head of the Commonwealth the Queen still takes considerable interest in them, however. Despite having no real political power, Queen Elizabeth is recognized as having a sound knowledge of politics, and her advice is well respected. The Queen's Silver Jubilee in 1977 was an occasion for great celebration throughout the country. Despite being one of the richest women in the world the Queen lives a relatively simple life, but has been troubled in latter years by the turbulent relationships of her children. Rumours that she may one day abdicate in favour of her son Charles have been circulated, but for the time being at least Queen Elizabeth II looks long set to continue.